THE ROLE OF THE MINISTER
IN A DYING CONGREGATION

Smyth & Helwys Publishing, Inc.
6316 Peake Road
Macon, Georgia 31210-3960
1-800-747-3016
©2011 by Smyth & Helwys Publishing
All rights reserved.
Printed in the United States of America.

The paper used in this publication meets the minimum requirements of
American National Standard for Information Sciences—
Permanence of Paper for Printed Library Materials.
ANSI Z39.48–1984. (alk. paper)

Library of Congress Cataloging-in-Publication Data

Jenkins, Lynwood B.
The role of the minister in a dying congregation / by Lynwood B. Jenkins.
p. cm.
Includes bibliographical references and index.
ISBN 978-1-57312-571-0 (pbk. : alk. paper)
1. Church closures.
2. Pastoral theology.
I. Title.
BV652.9.J46 2011
253—dc22

2010052891

THE ROLE OF THE

MINISTER IN A

DYING CONGREGATION

Lynwood B. Jenkins

To the many pastors and congregational leaders who are striving daily to discern the way ahead for their congregations in an ever-changing and increasingly diverse cultural context.

May you find encouragement for the journey from those who have already traveled this path.

ACKNOWLEDGMENTS

I wish to express my gratitude to my colleagues at the Baptist Theological Seminary at Richmond for their encouragement and support in this endeavor, and especially to Dr. Tracy L. Hartman for her wise counsel and thoughtful insight. I also offer a special word of thanks to Dr. Israel Galindo for his inspiration through writing, teaching, and dialogue.

This book would not have been possible without the generous gifts of time and energy from the leaders of Bainbridge Street Baptist Church and Weatherford Memorial Baptist Church. I am deeply appreciative of their willingness to share experiences and insights so that other congregations might benefit. I owe a debt of gratitude to the pastors who contributed immeasurably to my research— Dr. Ricky Hurst, Dr. Deborah Carlton Loftis, and Dr. Elmer West. I am also indebted to Rev. Glenn Akins, assistant executive director of the Virginia Baptist Mission Board, for his wise guidance, counsel, and insight early in my work.

I am thankful for all the colleagues and friends who have helped me to stay the course. The greatest gift of all has been the confidence, encouragement, support, and love I have received from my wife, Penny.

CONTENTS

## Chapter 1

LOOKING DOWN

Sunday morning worship concluded, the last person left the sanctuary, and I was ready to go home and enjoy a relaxing afternoon. Another challenging week of pastoral care demands from the aging congregation of Southampton Baptist Church had left me feeling drained. Instead of leaving, though, I hung up my coat and tie, grabbed paper and pen, and headed to the fellowship hall for lunch and a meeting with the study team.

I had urged the church to form this team of ten volunteers for the purpose of completing a study that would record the church's past, describe its present, and provide insight into its future. The team had worked for eight months collecting information, searching documents, and poring over records to amass a twenty-five-year history of the church. After sharing their study with a congregational health consultant and meeting with him twice to discuss their findings, they were now gathering to process what they had discovered. The consultant had confirmed their findings:

• membership had been declining for thirty years;
• there had been no baptisms in thirteen years;
• building maintenance expenses continued to increase;
• personnel expenses were the second largest budget item;
• mission efforts were minimal;

- decreasing income from tithes and offerings had been off-set by a 150 percent increase in rental income in order to continue to meet operating expenses;
- and designated giving had remained virtually unchanged during the same period.

The consultant's concluding remarks were honest and unambiguous. "This church," he said, "is in the last stage of the life cycle of a congregation." Our choices were limited:
- continue to operate as in the past and continue to decline until the church closes;
- envision and implement a radically different mission and ministry that every member could support and for which the members had the necessary energy;
- or determine how the church might leave a legacy and die with dignity.

Energy was essential for a new future. Did the church have the energy to envision and implement a radically new ministry? That was the question the study team was left to ponder.

As we gathered for our meeting, team members placed several tables together in a large rectangular shape and sat facing each other. We ate a simple meal of soup and bread. An atmosphere of anxiety hung over the room. Small talk during lunch quickly gave way to the much-anticipated question. The team leader broke the ice. "Death is a natural part of life," she said.

The response was immediate: "I have never given up hope." "I left those meetings with the consultant feeling very down. He was so negative. It was just depressing." *"I'm not ready to give up."* "I've talked to Mr. Smith from Main Street Baptist Church [names changed]. His church got one of those interns from the seminary, and she turned everything around. That's what I think we need to do. We need to get an intern who has lots of energy to come in here and revive our church." Others at the table nodded, affirming the suggestion that an intern would be the church's answer to reversing a thirty-year trend.

The team's reaction to the possibility of the congregation's death should not have surprised me. The most distinctive physical characteristic of the congregation was age. Most of our people were over seventy. Forty percent of the members were married, while another 35 percent were widowed. Sixty-five percent were female. Children and grandchildren occasionally attended worship on special family occasions or for Christmas and Easter services. There were no children or youth members. About one third of the members were employed, while the remaining members were living on their retirement income. The health of many members was poor. About 25 percent resided in nursing homes or were homebound. The members were all too aware of these realities, but not unlike our individual responses to the reality of our own mortality, organizational response to death is often resistance and denial.

Several leaders in the field of congregational health have identified and described the stages in the life of congregations (see Figure 1). George Barna suggests that the movement toward the end of a congregation's life can occur gradually, almost without the conscious awareness of the members.[1] This seemed to describe Southampton's experience well. Slowly, members who had been faithful participants moved away. Children grew, went to college, found jobs, and settled in other parts of the city or country. As the condition of the facilities declined, maintenance

Figure 1. Stages of Congregational Development[2]

Birth is the period of development when Vision is dominant, as core leaders form a congregation to fulfill a mission to a specific group of people or in a specific location.

Growth occurs as Vision moves the congregation to expand Relationships and attract more members, and develop Programs to meet identified needs, thus building the congregation.

Adulthood is achieved when Management and decision making share in the functioning of the congregation along with Vision, Relationships, and Programs. Everything is working at optimal levels.

Maturity is the stage when Vision is no longer a influential force as the congregation becomes more passive and less focused on the original core values.

Aging is a progressive stage when Vision, and Programs continue to fade from congregational life, finally joined by Relationships.

Death is the final stage when the aging process is not arrested and the congregation is sustained solely by Management in a limited capacity. The congregation is no longer a viable, functioning place of worship, mission, and fellowship.

increased, adding an ever-increasing burden to the church budget. Barna also observed,

> As is true in the business world, when a church experiences a period of intense hemorrhaging, death is the usual outcome. . . . In these churches little, if any, outreach or inreach takes place. The name and buildings may insinuate a church is present, but lives are not touched in a significant, spiritual way by such artifacts. As long as these churches have a handful of faithful attenders and can afford some meeting space and a speaker, they remain in existence. They have, however, essentially completed their life as a church.[3]

Southampton was a dying church, whether the members could accept that reality or chose to continue in denial. Alice Mann has written extensively about the nature of congregational life and health. She describes the experience of congregations entering the final stage of life in this way:

> If a congregation does attain both spiritual and institutional stability, it will always arrive at a moment when it is tempted to rest on it laurels. . . . At this point in the life-cycle curve, congregations resemble the cartoon coyote who speeds off the edge of a cliff and keeps going straight ahead from sheer momentum—until he looks down and discovers there is nothing under his feet! . . . At some point even the coyote realizes that he is falling. . . . After refusing for months, years, or even decades to "look down" at its situation, the congregation arrives at a moment of painful recognition.
>
> Unfortunately, the most common reaction is blame. . . . If a congregation never replaces the blame response with a learning stance, or if it waits too long to try something new, death is the likely result.[4]

Southampton's study team had looked down, but they were unable or unwilling to admit the depth of the congregation's fall.

The seriousness of the situation stunned me. I was the pastor of a congregation that could not help itself. What was my role as the pastor in this dying church? The question was not for me alone. As I began to explore resources that might be useful, I discovered the work of George W. Bullard Jr. I learned that fully 80 percent of churches in the United States are in at least the first stage of early aging as described by Bullard in his work on congregational life cycles.[5] (See Figure 1.)

A major element in understanding the life cycle of a congregation is to understand the pattern of the organizing principles that form the DNA and make up the various stages of congregational life. This life cycle is principle driven.[6] The organizing principles are . . .

Vision: The current understanding of God's spiritual strategic direction for a local congregation that is cast by the leadership and owned by the membership.

Relationships: The relational process by which persons are brought to faith in God through Jesus Christ; become connected to a local New Testament church; are assimilated into the fellowship, life, and care ministry of the church; have opportunities for spiritual growth and leadership development; and utilize their gifts and skills through Kingdom involvement.

Programs: The functional attempts to provide ministries, service, activities, and training for people connected to the congregation by membership, attendance, fellowship, or through relationship processes.

Management: The administration of the resources of the congregation, the decision-making structure of the congregation, the formal and informal culture of the congregation, and the openness of the congregation to change and grow.[7]

Bullard points out that churches who focus their energy on vision and relationships are the congregations that are continuously growing and expanding. These congregations are part of the 20 percent of churches in North America that are growing. Congregations that emphasize programs and management are becoming more passive and growing less vital with time.[8]

I found Bullard's model to be helpful as I considered the Southampton experience. Leadership and control were in the hands of a few longtime members. The church treasurer had served in that capacity for more than twenty-five years. A select group of tellers counted, recorded, and deposited the church receipts. The leader of the Women's Missionary Union (WMU) had personally managed an endowment fund for many years, using the interest to finance mission causes.

The programs and activities of the church were organized through the work of committees established by the constitution and bylaws. The church council, made up of representatives of each committee and organization, met monthly to discuss activities and plan the church calendar. Virtually all decisions and actions of the council were brought to the quarterly business meetings and approved by the congregation. Vision, relationships, and programs had essentially ceased to exist, with management consuming the attention and energy of the remaining members.

Churches in the declining stages of the life cycle face a daunting task. Israel Galindo wrote,

. . . The natural progression on the declining trajectory is
from the Maturity stage to the Bureaucracy stage [similar
to Bullard's *Aging* stage]. When a congregation slides out
of fully transitioning into this stage, it is well on the way
to dissolution; the likelihood of turning around a congregation in the grips of the hidden controlling life force
through renewal, revisioning, or pure force of will is
slim.[9]

The prospect of help and hope gained from the experiences
of other churches prodded me to explore this option further.
In the previous year I had begun work on my Doctor of
Ministry degree with the intent of using my experience in
what I hoped would be the revitalization of my church as
the focus of my doctoral project. As the possibility of this
happening at Southampton grew dimmer, I decided to shift
my attention to exploring the experiences of churches that
had undergone the painful but necessary process of realistic
self-examination.

Self-examination tools like those included in the appendix were not available to me at the time, but they would
have been helpful as I struggled to make sense of
Southhampton's situation. I began by asking myself, "Where
do pastors of dying churches turn for answers?"

One congregation near Southampton was able to bring
their ministry to a positive end, leaving behind a meaningful
legacy. Another nearby congregation sold their property and
dispersed, leaving virtually no trace of their former existence.
I wondered if their experiences could inform the situation
we faced at Southampton Baptist Church. In the following
pages, I will share the details of my search for answers.

Questions to Consider

In answering these questions (and the other questions that appear at the end of each chapter), you may consider using the assessment tools found in the appendix.

1. When did your church last complete a self-study? What did you learn at that time? What has changed since then? Is it time to do another study?

2. Is your church tempted to rest on its laurels? What indications do you see of this tendency?

3. After reading this chapter, where in the life cycle is your church? Would the staff and congregation agree with your assessment? What are your plans to give them the opportunity to provide their insights?

Notes

1. George Barna, *Turn around Churches: How to Overcome Barriers to Growth and Bring New Life to an Established Church* (Ventura CA: Regal Books, 1993) 19–22.

2. George Bullard Jr., *Pursuing the Full Kingdom Potential of Your Congregation* (St. Louis: Lake Hickory Resources, 2005) 96.

3. George Barna, *Turn around Churches: How to Overcome Barriers to Growth and Bring New Life to an Established Church* (Ventura CA: Regal Books, 1993) 22–23.

4. Alice Mann, *Can Our Church Live?: Redeveloping Congregations in Decline* (Bethesda MD: Alban Institute, 1999) 6–7.

5. Shared in an oral presentation by Glenn Akins of the Virginia Baptist Mission Board, Richmond VA, to the study team at Southampton Baptist Church on 29 October 2006.

6. Bullard, *Pursuing the Full Kingdom Potential of Your Congregation*, 96.

7. Ibid., 76–77.

8. Ibid., 77.

9. Israel Galindo, *The Hidden Lives of Congregations: Understanding Congregational Dynamics* (Herndon VA: The Alban Institute, 2004) 73–74.

## Chapter 2

BEING CHURCH

"In the common life we are to seek to be a true community of faith, manifesting the community bond in corporate worship, mutual edification, and outreach to the world."[1]

I wondered what had slipped away from the faithful few in my congregation. To be a viable community of faith, the church must be real; it must be authentic; it must be rooted in and living out a sound ecclesiology. What was missing? What had been lost? What was never there all along? A beginning point for me was to look honestly at the purpose and function of the church. I knew that any real help for me, or for pastors leading other dying congregations, must begin there.

The church gathers as a community of faith to worship God. We Christians are to love God absolutely and completely so that whenever we gather, this purpose stands at the core of our being. The Bible is the foundation and source of guidance for our faith and practice as a Christian community. Scripture informs our identity, both individually and corporately, as a people whose purpose is to worship and glorify God and to love others. In Matthew's Gospel, we read,

> [Jesus] said to him, "'You shall love the Lord your God with all your heart, and with all your soul, and with all

your mind.' This is the greatest and first commandment. And a second is like it: 'You shall love your neighbor as yourself.' On these two commandments hang all the law and the prophets." (Matt 22:37-40 NRSV)[2]

Equally important to worship is Jesus' commandment that his followers are to love their neighbors as they love themselves. This is particularly true as we care for those whom Christ considered the least among them. Jesus declared, "Truly I tell you, just as you did it to one of the least of these who are members of my family, you did it to me" (Matt 25:40).

When any church begins, core concepts help shape the life of the congregation. Alice Mann asserts that a new church begins immediately to define itself.

> During this time, the congregation develops its own tacit answers to three powerful questions:
> 1. Who are we (especially at a faith level)?
> 2. What are we here for?
> 3. Who is our neighbor?
>   . . . As congregations are born and develop, their answer to the third formative question—"Who is our neighbor?"—flows from the other two.[3]

The imprint this initial process makes on every congregation tends to be a lasting one. I was certain this was true at my church. I knew their history and had heard their stories. They had begun the church in what was once the clubhouse of a golf course. Homes were springing up in new neighborhoods as middle-income and upper-middle-income families moved from the city to what were the suburbs in the mid-1950s. They built the church and the people came.

Mann's questions helped me better understand how my church and others develop a unique character and personality. Through worship, which includes proclamation, and through corporate and individualized education, churches answer the first two questions. Their response to the third question shapes how the church will reach out to the world. Israel Galindo insists that the way a church relates to the world is of foremost importance.

> The primary mandate of the church is to be a transforming influence in the world. This is how the church becomes relevant in people's lives. The institutional tendency of organizations, however, is to focus primarily on self-preservation and on the comfort and benefit of their own members. And while a congregation is an institutionalized expression of the Church, it is wrong, and against its nature, when self-preservation and comfort become the primary reasons for its existence.[4]

Galindo's words had a stinging truth for me. Obviously, institutional behavior that is too inwardly focused has the potential to negatively affect the health and vitality of a congregation as it ages. I could see that all too clearly in my own congregation: When visitors attended the worship service, members welcomed them, but they often commented later, "they [the visitors] were nice people, but they're just not like us." On another occasion when a visitor in a wheelchair began attending regularly, I proposed modifying the seating space in the sanctuary by removing a pew to accommodate the wheelchair. This idea was rejected because it would have required changing the original design of the worship space. Such a change was considered unacceptable, even though it would have greatly benefited this visitor and his family.

Historically, had churches shifted their purpose from outward (being a transforming influence) to inward (preserving the comfort of their members)? I decided to take a backward glance at how churches defined themselves in the past. Craig Van Gelder's work proved to be instructive. In *The Essence of the Church: A Community Created by the Spirit*, he traces the historical views of the church as they developed over the centuries, leading to an institutional tendency. The Nicene Creed and the Apostles' Creed shaped the view of the church for centuries. Van Gelder wrote,

> The church of the fourth century viewed itself as being one, holy, catholic, and apostolic. It was a unified and visible social community that existed in a relational and organizational unity throughout the world, displayed the presence of God, and exercised apostolic authority on his behalf through the office of bishop.[5]

The Protestant Reformation ushered in a new period of the ongoing development of how the church defined itself. There was a shift from apostolic authority to biblical authority and to the establishment of state churches, all of which had a dramatic impact. Van Gelder continued,

> In place of papal authority, these churches developed confessional standards and church politics to guide the practices of the church. . . . Explicit within their approach was the priority given to the institutional character of the church. Attention focused on the authority of the institutional church for ministering the means of grace through preaching and sacraments. . . . The organizational life of the church, which came to be known as church polity, was structured around insuring that these

responsibilities were performed decently and in good order.[6]

The free-church movement came into being during this Reformation period, offering an alternative expression of church than the state church approach. Free-church advocates were committed to the separation of church and state, the personal conversion experience of the believer, and the membership of the community consisting of professing believers. Although never dominant in their initial European context, many of these characteristics would emerge in the development of denominations in North America during the eighteenth and nineteenth centuries.[7]

Van Gelder points to pietism, mission societies, and the modern missions movement as the next significant influences on ecclesiology. An emphasis on personal piety contributed to the view of missions as the work of specialized persons within the church. Missions became a primary responsibility of the church, supported and conducted by specific groups in the local church. The result was a shift toward personal discipleship and the view of missions as the work of a few designated persons.[8]

As I followed Van Gelder's historical journey through the centuries, I began to see more clearly how these shifts affected the answers to Alice Mann's questions—those questions every church uses to define itself ("Who are we?" "What are we here for?" "Who is our neighbor?").

This shift had another effect on ministry within the church. With a greater emphasis on personal piety came a lessening of the importance of ordained clergy as the sole means for the administration of grace. This movement toward personal piety not only undercut the authority of the established churches in Europe but also contributed to the creation of numerous missions entities. William Carey and others sought and received support to carry out their missions endeavors directly from the churches themselves. Churches no longer viewed the work of missions as their exclusive purview, directly related to the question, "What are we here for?" According to Van Gelder,

> These newly created missional structures became the primary organizational form through which European churches engaged in missions over the next century. Their North American equivalents became the parachurch and faith-missions structures, along with denominational boards and agencies.[9]

The struggle of the free-church movement in England contributed further to the concept of a denominational church. Not surprisingly, in response to persecution and attempts to squelch their movement, churches sought a theological basis for their existence. This goes to the heart of the question, "Who are we?"

To answer this question, efforts were made to rediscover the core components of the New Testament church, coupled with the conviction that the visible unity of the church was more important than theological and organizational differences. This new form for church became widely accepted in the American colonies where diversity of structure and traditions contributed to a dynamic mix. Denominationalism resulted.[10]

The influence of the Enlightenment furthered the development of this new form of church. Thinkers such as John Locke desired to provide a new theory for the structure of society. Locke believed society was properly seen as voluntary in character. The church quickly began to be viewed as an organization of society constituted by persons who voluntarily chose to gather. Today, many see the church as a voluntary organization gathered along denominational lines. This, according to Van Gelder, profoundly impacts "the nature, ministry, and organization of the church."[11]

There they are again. Van Gelder's analysis of the evolution of the church kept returning me to those same three questions posed by Mann. We can see the consequences of the denominational structure in the attention given to developing strategies designed to satisfy the membership so they would choose not to leave the church. Efforts to improve and enhance the organizational delivery system became the church's objective. The church came to be viewed more and more like an organization, although there were variations in structures and procedures among denominations.[12] Most congregations may not perceive of themselves in this way, but observation of a routine business meeting will quickly confirm the reality of this description.

If the church has become more like an organization, then is it not reasonable to expect that it will exhibit organizational traits? We know from our own experience that one characteristic of all organizations is the natural process of aging. Martin Saarinen credits Ichak Adizes with inspiring his work on congregational life cycles: "Adizes used the analogy of stages in human development to explain the rise and fall of organizations. . . . There is much fertile ground to be plowed in transplanting these notions in the soil of the church organization, particularly the local congregation."[13]

All congregations will proceed through a congregational life cycle. The length of that cycle may vary dramatically from a few years to hundreds of years. Saarinen and those authorities on congregational life I mentioned earlier (Barna,

Mann, and Bullard) have developed models that depict this natural progression. A church that fails to revitalize will continue to decline to a point where it will become impossible to sustain congregational health.

In Bullard's model, a key element in congregational vitality is vision. According to the writer of Proverbs, "Where there is no vision, the people perish" (Prov 29:18a, KJV). As those who were part of the original formation of the congregation age and die, the tendency is toward a loss of the original vision. Newer members can grasp a new vision or recast the original vision, but without such action the church will continue to decline.

Keith Spencer, a Lutheran pastor and contributor to *Ending with Hope: A Resource for Closing Congregations*, observes,

> In many communities, our homes and churches are at risk, and it is time for us to ask ourselves a question of great significance: What is God calling us to do in this place? . . . Discerning what God is calling us to do as a congregation might appear on the surface to have little to do with congregational viability. . . . Unfortunately, too many congregations put off conversations about viability until there are no longer choices to be made. They use silence as an escape from growing fears that the congregation may be dying.[14]

Silence does not alter the course of a congregation through the stages of its life any more than amnesia does. The congregation's ability to grapple with these challenges will depend heavily on strong leadership.

The role of the pastor is critical to the life of any congregation. Robert Dale defines the role of the pastor as three-fold:

> Broadly described, Christian ministry calls on us [pas-
> tors] to (1) proclaim the gospel to believers and
> unbelievers by means of preaching and worship as well as
> evangelism and nurture, (2) care for the church's mem-
> bers and other persons in the community through
> pastoral counseling and visitation as well as family min-
> istries and grief support, and (3) lead the church in
> achievement of its mission. Proclaim, care, and lead.
> That's the functional baseline for ministry.[15]

Perhaps the greatest challenge for the pastor of the dying
church comes in the fulfillment of the leadership role.
Leading a congregation to achieve their mission (outreach to
the world) necessitates a clear understanding of and commitment to the vision (how the congregation defines and
reaches out to its neighbors). The task of casting that vision
still resides with the pastor. Galindo emphasizes this pivotal
leadership role.

> There is nothing more critical to a congregation's
> integrity than its pastor's ability to provide vision.
> While we generally refer to leadership as a corporate
> function that rests on the position of the pastor and lay
> leaders, vision is a systemic function that is the pastor's
> prerogative.[16]

The expectation when casting a vision is that there are
those who are willing and able to receive it. In a church in
the declining stages of life, members may have become emo-
tionally unwilling or physically unable to engage in
revisioning the church. Invariably the foci become the
weekly worship service, occasional fellowship gatherings,
and an increasingly nostalgic view of the past. Maintenance
of the traditions of the church and the familiar patterns of

worship and fellowship take priority. I often heard elderly
members of the Southampton congregation express the sentiment that they had "done their duty" or were "worn out"
from years of serving the church. Saarinen describes this
tendency in this way: "Inertia . . . has [a] ripple effect
throughout the whole organism, affecting its processes and
structures in a progressively crippling manner from stage to
stage."[17]

The crippling process has another disturbing consequence. Pastoral tenure is negatively affected. In his article,
"Why Churches Die," David Padfield comments on what he
has witnessed in dead congregations:

> Dead congregations usually have a history of "short-term"
> preachers, i.e., men [sic] who only stay two or three years
> before moving on. Sometimes this is because the men
> they asked to work with them are lazy. . . . Sometimes
> churches have a high turnover of preachers because the
> church is full of knuckleheads and unrepentant sinners
> (cf. 3 John 1:9-10). I know of a few congregations who
> have had five preachers in the past ten years—some men
> did not even stay a full year. When the truth is taught
> and the local Diotrephes gets his toes stepped on, the eas-
> iest thing to do is to kill the messenger (cf. Acts 7:54-60).
> Bickering among brethren is an infectious disease (James
> 3:1-12). Neglect in the pulpit usually results in a lack of
> stability in a congregation and no consistency in public
> teaching.[18]

Glenn Akins, assistant executive director of the Virginia
Baptist Mission Board, knew of no research that could doc-
ument an actual shortening of pastoral tenure in dying
congregations, but he did describe a recurring response
among congregations that have not yet accepted their con-

gregational decline. Churches in this stage of the life cycle feel the need for a scapegoat—someone on whom they can cast the responsibility for the congregation's situation. They go through a period of blaming and dismissing pastors in an attempt to remedy their problem. Akins contends that these congregations pass through this stage and move into a final stage where they seek a "chaplain" to care for the members and stay, often for a lengthy time, "until death do us part."[19] Pastors who work in such congregations may also become exhausted by the heavy demands of an aging and dwindling congregation—frequent funerals, an extraordinarily high demand for home and hospital visits, and a shortage of physically able and willing workers for the routine tasks of ministry within the life of the congregation. During my first eighteen months at Southampton, I conducted or assisted in the funerals of fourteen members of the church.

Paul Lamey, in his online posting on *Expository Thoughts* titled "Length of Tenure," observes, "The average tenure of a pastor in the US is three years. That's despicable and horrific when we consider what it takes to effectively minister to God's flock in the way that He has prescribed."[20] Regardless of the reason for short tenures, when pastoral leadership changes every three years, the visionary role of the pastor becomes daunting. Israel Galindo observes,

> A genuine vision is unique to each congregation—even while all congregations everywhere share the same mission. . . . This is also why pastors cannot begin to formulate a vision until well into their fifth year of ministry at the church. . . . Until a pastor has been at a congregation for at least five years, he or she does not know the congregation well enough to shape a vision. It takes that long to get to know the hidden life of the con-

gregation and to get clear about one's necessary leadership function in that particular context.[21]

A real quandary can arise for a pastor. I had been at Southampton for a little more than three years. I began to have serious questions about the church and its viability. Can the congregation remain viable long enough for me to acquire the needed knowledge and build the necessary relationships to discern and cast a vision? Simultaneously, I wondered if the present congregation might have fulfilled its original calling in that place and should simply conclude its ministry with dignity and grace. The author of Ecclesiastes tells us, "For everything there is a season, and a time for every matter under heaven: a time to be born, and a time to die; a time to plant, and a time to pluck up what is planted" (Eccl 3:1-2). I began to observe a tendency among members of dying congregations to assert that the local church simply cannot die. The death of a congregation would imply that God had somehow abandoned the church.

Tanya Stormo Rasmussen recounts some of the questions her parishioners voiced as they struggled with the closing of their church:

> Are we a failure or disappointment to God? Has God given up on us? Is God "with" the "successful" churches in a way that God is not "with" us? Do the bigger, more active churches glorify God more faithfully than we do? Am I a personal failure in faith if I am associated with a church that cannot seem to stay alive on its own? What does it say about God's faithfulness to us—if we die (as a congregation), even after trying to live, does it mean God has abandoned or stopped loving us?[22]

These are not uncommon questions among member of dying congregations. Churches are supposed to be as everlasting as God's faithfulness to God's people. Although the sentiment is sincere, the contemporary reality in North American church life does not support such a view. Gilson Waldkoenig notes that researchers portray a sobering picture:

> Overall, researchers' findings are consistent. The Hartford study found that over 50 percent of North American congregations had fewer than 100 regularly participating adults in worship each week. Lyle Schaller calculated that over half of Protestant churches in America had fewer than 100 in worship on an average Sunday, and two-thirds had fewer than 75. . . . Religion writer David Yount cites fewer than 75 members for half of the nation's churches. Yount asserts that "these churches are dying at the rate of 50 every week in America."[23]

In *Missional Church: A Vision for the Sending of the Church in North America*, Craig Van Gelder and the other authors develop their views of the plight of the church in North America and their vision . . . and proclaim the reign of God to the world.[24] The loss of denominational identity, an emphasis on attracting the unchurched and reengaging the inactive members, and a changing cultural context have altered the composition of the churches in North America. Alan Roxburgh posits that

> . . . more and more churches [are] filled with people who have little sense of a cohesive belief system. People enter churches with undifferentiated assortments of beliefs— some often quite vague—garnered from a mixture of

sources. They enter also as individual consumers looking for churches that meet personal needs.[25]

Roxburgh describes this church using three concentric circles. Within the center circle (A) resides the committed core of the church composed of the faithful and active people. The second circle (B) represents the larger congregation, including the core group. This group is primarily composed of those who consume services from the leadership and core members. The third circle (C) defines the context of the church where the unchurched and seekers are found. The line between the core and the congregation is a solid one, indicating a clear separation between these two groups. The line between the second and third circles is dotted, suggesting that the distinction between the consumer congregation and the unchurched is blurred.[26]

This is not a description of the missional church called and sent to witness to and proclaim the reign of God to the world. As the human and material resources of the core continue to diminish, and the "gospel" is further refashioned in an attempt to attract the inactive and unchurched within the church's context, these congregations continue their steady decline. When the local church is no longer the "called and sent," when there is no longer a "witness to and proclamation of the reign of God in the world," radical measures may be necessary. Jesus said, "Very truly, I tell you, unless a grain of wheat falls into the earth and dies, it remains just a single grain; but if it dies, it bears much fruit" (John 12:24). Is it not possible that, in dying, these churches may follow the example of their Lord by unselfishly giving themselves away? Can the fruits of such deliberate acts of sacrifice multiply the

Figure 2. The Relationship between the Culture and the Church[27]

The energies of leaders are dissipated, first, in meeting the needs of individuals within the core and affiliates segments of the congregation (A and B), and second, shaping the congregation's ethos to meet the needs of those in the context who are not yet in the congregation. The focal energy of leadership is directed toward getting people in the center, A, but the location where the leader expends most of his or [her] time and energy is in circles B and C. All this assumes a reductionistic gospel of meeting personal, individualistic needs.[28]

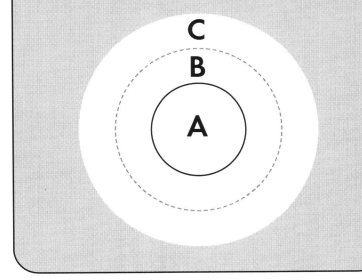

witness and proclamation of God's reign in new and relevant ways?

The work of leading a congregation through this self-realization and discernment process is part of the task of pastoral leadership in a dying congregation. The message of the authentic Hebrew prophets was never a popular one among the people. The biblical record abounds with the stories of reluctant prophets. Yet, God called and sent those messengers to lead the people into uncertain futures, and those prophets responded. God still calls and sends messengers to God's people.

Pastors in dying churches are faced with the competing roles of proclamation, care, and leadership. They are further challenged by the unique cultural context the church faces today. In Roxburgh's view,

> Making a transition from the optimism of modernity to the humility of a people in exile evokes the experience of brokenness. Voicing this brokenness enables churches to feel the gulf between their present forms and the covenant community of Jesus. Evoking this voice is a deeply pastoral task.[29]

Pastors who have led their churches through the process of ending a congregation's ministry and closing can provide valuable insights and advice to those for whom this task remains. Important questions arise with regard to what selective pastoral care approaches are effective: What combinations of care and nurture work best? What forms of worship and preaching work well? What education and self-study programs assist the members in moving forward while appropriately acknowledging the past? I found answers to these and other questions as I explored the experience of these seasoned practitioners. Their answers may be used to better inform and equip pastors and congregational leaders for ministry with dying congregations.

Questions to Consider

In answering these questions, you may consider using the assessment tools found in the appendix, particularly the "Ministries Assessment."

1. How does your congregation answer the question, "Who is our neighbor?"
2. What is your church's vision? How do your people answer the question, "What are we here for?"
3. Who casts the vision in your church?
4. How would you characterize the level of energy your congregation is willing and able to commit to the tasks required to accomplish their vision and mission?

Notes

1. Stanley J. Grenz, *Theology for the Community of God* (Grand Rapids MI: W. B. Eerdmands, 2000) 490.

2. All subsequent quotations of Scripture will be from the NRSV unless otherwise noted.

3. Alice Mann, *Can Our Church Live?: Redeveloping Congregations in Decline* (Bethesda MD: Alban Institute, 1999) 3–4.

4. Israel Galindo, *The Hidden Lives of Congregations: Understanding Congregational Dynamics* (Herndon VA: The Alban Institute, 2004) 41.

5. Craig Van Gelder, *The Essence of the Church: A Community Created by the Spirit* (Grand Rapids: Baker Books, 2000) 51.

6. Ibid., 55–56.

7. Ibid., 59–60.

8. Ibid., 61–63.

9. Ibid., 63.

10. Ibid., 66.

11. Ibid., 67.

12. Ibid., 68–69.

13. Martin F. Saarinen, *The Life Cycle of a Congregation* (Washington DC: The Alban Institute, 1990) 3.

14. Keith Spencer, "Assessing Congregational Viability," in *Ending with Hope: A Resource for Closing Congregations*, ed. Beth Ann Gaede (Bethesda MD: The Alban Institute, 2002) 18.

15. Robert D. Dale, *Pastoral Leadership: A Handbook of Resources for Effective Congregational Leadership* (Nashville: Abingdon Press, 1986) 17.

16. Galindo, 139–40.

17. Saarinen, 15.

18. David Padfield, "Why Churches Die," Zion IL, 1998.

19. Glenn Akins, interview by author, Richmond VA, 13 February 2008.

20. Paul Lamey, "Length of Tenure," 20 February 2006, http://expository-thoughts.wordpress.com/2006/02/20/length-of-tenure/ (accessed 13 February 2008).

21. Galindo, 143.

22. Tanya Stormo Rasmussen, "The Members' Experience," in *Ending with Hope: A Resource for Closing Congregations*, ed. Beth Ann Gaede (Bethesda MD: The Alban Institute, 2002) 47.

23. Gilson A. C. Waldkoenig, "Closing Churches in the Light of American Religious History," in *Ending with Hope*, 39–40.

24. Lois Barrett, Inagrace T. Dietterich, Darrell L. Guder, George R. Hunsberger, Alan J. Roxburgh, and Craig Van Gelder, *Missional Church: A Vision for the Sending of the Church in North America*, ed. Darrell L. Guder (Grand Rapids MI: W. B. Eerdmans Pub., 1998).

25. Ibid., 201.

26. Ibid., 202–203.

27. Ibid., 202.

28. Ibid., 203.

29. Ibid., 200.

## Chapter 3

LEARNING FROM OTHERS

JUMP-STARTING THE REALITY CHECK

Early in my conversations with pastors who had participated in helping congregations conclude their ministries, I learned that lay leaders were crucial in this process. These key leaders are often the best equipped to assist in identifying ways to honor the past and invest in the future. Timing is critical in this process, a point that Alice Mann affirms.

> Sometimes a congregation dies because it has completed its task, or because a changed environment is now calling forth an entirely different kind of ministry. What would constitute a holy death in that situation? The hospice movement has helped many individuals to make their last months both dignified and emotionally rich, but this cannot happen if the person keeps waiting for a cure. When a congregation faces its impending death sooner, while there are still enough members around for a wonderful "funeral" event, the concluding days of that faith community can be spiritually powerful. Bestowing a financial legacy on some other ministry that carries forward the congregation's values can provide an additional sense of self-esteem and continuity.[1]

Congregations might not be open to listening to the pastor, especially if she or he is relatively new, but they might be open to hearing the voices of experience, the trusted lay leaders. This may make it possible for the members to face the question of death sooner. The size and impact of the financial legacy a congregation leaves are often influenced significantly by the timing of that congregation's actions. Churches that anguish over closing, putting the bulk of their financial resources into remaining open as long as possible, can deplete virtually all resources without producing any tangible benefits. Likewise, the remaining members can expend precious emotional and spiritual energy attempting to protect the church from the perceived encroachment of a changing community, all the while failing to grasp opportunities for outreach right on their doorstep.

I could see this unfolding clearly in my own congregation. The building and furnishings continued to deteriorate, both cosmetically and structurally. As the cost of maintenance spiraled upward, more and more money was needed only to accomplish less and less. The once-thriving day care center at the church had been closed years ago, and more recently the space had been rented to an agency that provided services to special-needs children who were bused in from around the city. The benefit of this arrangement for the congregation was that the rental income bolstered the church budget, while also ensuring the ongoing maintenance and repair of the rented space. But what would happen if this source of financial support disappeared?

My research suggested that there were better options for churches. Beth Ann Gaede observed,

. . . although closing a congregation is in many ways about dying, it can also be about new life. The closing of some churches and the movement of those people to both new and established congregations can be a source of revitalization for the receiving congregations. By closing one congregation, energy is released for use in places where God is working in new ways.[2]

I realized that dying congregations, whether they have the capacity to leave a legacy or not, should have the opportunity to obtain relevant counsel and advice for the process they face. This realization compelled me to interview key individuals who were actually involved in the closing of churches. In the course of these conversations, I discovered pastoral and lay leadership activities and strategies that both supported and inhibited the transition process for these congregations. Analyzing their experiences, I discovered practices and actions that could help other congregations conclude their ministries in the most appropriate way for their individual situations.

I conducted most of my interviews with the former members of two Richmond congregations that had recently closed. I also interviewed a pastor and an associate pastor from two congregations that closed in the 1980s. My purpose was three-fold: (1) to determine what process the churches had followed in concluding their ministries; (2) to seek participants' evaluations of the effectiveness of the process; and (3) to explore the role of the pastors in helping the churches end their ministries. The following interview questions were asked of all interviewees.

• When/at what point did you realize that the church was not going to survive/live or wasn't viable?

- What did you do to make the process flow better toward closure?
- Did it help? How? Why or why not?
- What would you do differently, given the opportunity?
- Were there some things you did that you believe ought to be done by other churches facing this situation?
- Were there things you did that you believe ought not to be done?
- What helped you come to an understanding of the situation and allowed you to move forward personally?
- What enabled you to help others/the church move forward?
- Was anything done, or not done, that diverted attention away from the ultimate resolution of the situation the church faced?
- Imagine that you go to sleep and wake up to find that the perfect way of doing this process is in place. What would it look like?
- What one thing would you *absolutely do* again?
- What one thing would you *absolutely not do* again?
- How important is time? How much time was needed to work through the process? Did you devote enough time? Too much? Too little?

The closing of a congregation was at one time a seldom-witnessed occurrence. You and I know that this is no longer the case. A disinterested observer's understanding of what that event might be like is profoundly different from that of a congregational member or staff person. I admit that I began this process with a degree of openness to what I might discover, but with some underlying expectations. My many conversations with participants in the closing of the four unique congregations, spanning more than twenty years, revealed both confirmations and revelations.

THE CASE OF WEATHERFORD MEMORIAL BAPTIST CHURCH

Weatherford Memorial Baptist Church was organized on February 3, 1907, composed of 146 former members of Clopton Street Church and 10 new members from the community around 2807 Hull Street, south of Richmond, Virginia, in Chesterfield County.[3] The church thrived in that location, prompting the members to purchase property in 1948 at McGuire Circle and Hull Street. This new location would become the home of Weatherford from 1953 until it closed in 2005.

The 1950s and 1960s were times of growth and outreach in their new community, but dramatic change for the church came with the 1970s. "'. . . [C]hurch membership and attendance began to decline after the city annexed the area around Weatherford in 1970,' several Weatherford members said. 'There was court-ordered busing and the white flight began.'"[4]

Weatherford would not close until September 2005, but several of the congregation's senior members looked back to the 1970s as the time when change began. One member observed that there were twelve to fourteen babies in the nursery when she first began attending in the 1950s. During the 1973–1974 church year, there were only two babies in the nursery. "The church was changing," the member told me. "Children were mixed-race." Although attempts were made to reach the changing community, including door-to-door visitation, the gap between the congregation and the community only widened. By the late 1980s and early 1990s, cars were being stolen from the church parking lot during Wednesday evening and Sunday morning services, necessitating the institution of a system of parking lot supervision by the men of the church.

The signs of congregational distress were more readily discernable at times of pastoral transition. "Every time a pastor left, members would leave," noted one former leader. Others began to doubt the church's future viability when pastoral initiatives were resisted. One of the last pastors attempted to institute changes in the worship service, to increase community outreach efforts, and to focus congregational resources on becoming a ministry center for the community. His efforts were resisted, ultimately resulting in his resignation. He declared upon leaving that the church "wouldn't make it."

The realization that the church would not survive was a gradual process. "People were leaving the church. No new, younger members were joining. Some [church] activities were stopped," noted one member. These events were significant turning points toward closure.

"Process" is a word that the final pastor used to describe what he went through as he came to understand that the church was dying. In a seminary class, one of the pastor's professors helped him see that he needed to look at the situation at his church objectively. In the professor's words, "Your church is dying and you are sent there to help them have a good death." Over the next year, the pastor "processed" this concept. As he explained it to me, he came to see that he "needed to be instrumental in moving them toward a decision and an action. My objective was that they have a good ending."

To this end, this pastor initiated an intentional process. He began to "press the church to do their very best, in hopes that they would realize they didn't have what it would take to do the ministry needed in the community." The plan would unfold over three years, beginning in 2002 with a church-wide focus on spirituality. The following year the members worked on an evaluation of the church's resources and context. By 2004, goal setting and implementation was scheduled to begin, but catastrophe struck with the devastating impact of a hurricane.

Hurricane Gaston caused visible flooding throughout Richmond, but for Weatherford the result was the less obvious collection of approximately 33,000 gallons of water under the sanctuary. This created a problem with mold and required the evacuation of the space for six months while massive repairs were undertaken. The consequences of this natural disaster were far reaching. Some members left when the sanctuary was closed for repair, and those who stayed began to look at the church and its resources in a different light. A number of things could have prompted this new perspective, according to the pastor, because "the roof and the air conditioner needed replacing."

Not long after this crisis unfolded, a new resource became available at the Virginia Baptist Mission Board (VBMB). Reverend Glenn Akins joined the VBMB staff as congregational transformation/church growth consultant. Akins was invited to meet with key leaders at Weatherford to review the church's history and current situation. He was completely honest, telling the leaders "they needed to consider how to end well and leave a legacy."

When asked what they had done to make the process toward closure flow more smoothly, those interviewed provided a variety of responses. "Trying to stay positive" was the simple response of one key leader. One couple became active on the two primary committees formed by the congregation to investigate future courses of action. The husband served on the physical facility committee while the wife worked on the congregational issues committee. Akins spoke with these committees and later to the whole congregation. As this couple remembered the events, "Nothing really happened until Glenn Akins came to speak to the congregation. The congregation needed outside help."

Another couple recalled their efforts at trying to "keep the main thing the main thing." The members of Weatherford Memorial had a clear vision when they chose to move to the church's present location. Originally, the members of Weatherford wanted to be a "lighthouse to South Richmond." This vision was resurrected as this couple determined to help the church return to that focus. Their mantra became, "How do we make this church become a lighthouse to South Richmond once again?"

Everyone I interviewed affirmed that God was an active participant in the process. Allowing events to take their course was not so much a passive stance as it was an acknowledgment that what was happening was "a God thing." As one leader put it, "The Lord had a hand in this."

The pace of the process was seen as a positive contributing factor. The leaders took time to consider alternatives, explore various options, and allow people to express their different views. This ultimately allowed the members to resolve many of their early differences and emotional reactions to proposals.

Several leaders volunteered their view of the pastor's role in the process, affirming that the pastor was a "great guy" but disagreeing about his approach during the process of closing. One couple felt that the pastor "lacked pastoral leadership. The congregation never knew where the pastor stood." He "needed to cast a vision," and had failed to do so. A second couple expressed an almost opposite view that "the pastor was the right person for the task. Being patient in the midst of death was his practice." Interestingly, these key leaders had all observed the pastor's actions in exactly the same committee meetings and congregational gatherings. When the pastor was asked whether his actions had helped during the closing process, he acknowledged that "every situation is probably different," but what had happened at Weatherford Memorial "was something of God." He recognized that the congregation could not go on as it was, without the essential zeal and physical energy required for the task of ministry in their changed and changing context. If what he did helped the process along, he was reticent to take any credit, rather saying, "if anything [I was] sometimes a willing and sometimes an unwilling instrument."

Most of the leaders would not do anything differently, given the opportunity. One couple acknowledged that they would have been more compassionate to others, prayed more, listened to God more, and been more proactive in seeking the pastor's input and leadership. They believed other churches in similar situations ought to "remain focused," "keep the main thing the main thing," and "not let petty issues create unnecessary problems."

There was consensus that bringing in an outside resource was instrumental in helping them make a decision. Representatives of the area denominational association and state denominational leaders had visited Weatherford Memorial in the past. However, as one leader put it, "Glenn Akins helped as much as anything."

For the pastor, the church-wide spiritual evaluation he instituted proved to be helpful in preparing the congregation for the decisions that lay ahead. Members were asked to evaluate their own spiritual energy as well as the energy of the larger church community. The results of this evaluation were not positive, revealing a number of significant issues about the future viability of the congregation. In the pastor's view, these results may have been the catalyst in the process of closing Weatherford.

Reverend Akins had told the Weatherford members that another congregation might have an interest in the church property. St. Paul's Baptist Church, located east of Richmond, was a large, growing African-American congregation. Many members of St. Paul's lived in the communities surrounding Weatherford. Akins turned to this congregation with information about the Weatherford situation. When St. Paul's agreed to accept the gift of the facility, the leaders could see God at work. "No one else could have accomplished what St. Paul's could. It was 'a God thing,'" one leader observed.

Coming to a personal understanding of what was happening helped all these individuals, but they were also asked what enabled them to help others in the congregation move ahead. Two couples believed that seeing God at work in the events enabled them to help other members.

One couple expressed their amazement that the congregation ultimately voted to give the facility away. "Truly, I didn't believe God could do it. God accomplished what God wanted in spite of people."

I asked the leaders if anything was done that diverted attention away from closing the church once the congregation made that decision. Having a substantial endowment fund and owning two residential properties near the church had been distracting the members from an acceptance of their overall financial situation. Once issues concerning the disposition of these assets were resolved, those involved were freed to concentrate on concluding the active ministry of Weatherford Memorial.

My interviews with the leadership of Weatherford Memorial took place slightly more than two years after the final worship service on September 25, 2005. Given the advantage of hindsight, I asked the leaders if they could envision a "perfect way" to bring the ministry of a congregation to a close.

One couple imagined a "congregation on their knees, crying out to God, with lots of prayer meetings, sharing from the heart, seeking God's will, and continuing until they get an answer." Another couple suggested that bringing in an "outside expert" sooner and focusing on how the church can best leave a legacy would be important for other congregations.

When I asked the pastor, he shared that several critical things must happen for a church to consider concluding its ministry and closing. The pastor, key leaders, and the congregation must come to the realization that it is time to conclude the church's ministry. And one more thing must happen—something catastrophic must occur. To come to this realization, each person must understand the congregation in its context: Who are they? Who are their neighbors? What do they need to be doing? The catastrophe for Weatherford Memorial was the accumulation of water under the sanctuary after Hurricane Gaston. But the catastrophe for other churches need not be a natural disaster. It can be something as ordinary as the need to replace the roof or the air conditioner. Given this information, a church is much more likely to comprehend its situation and take the appropriate action.

Weatherford Memorial made the decision to close in September 2004 and held its last service in September 2005. Some leaders felt that they had prolonged the process, convinced that six months would have been adequate. Others believed that the process should not be rushed, and that taking lots of time and holding lots of meetings was not inappropriate.

"Time is important. Patience is needed," the pastor told me. From his perspective, the process had begun three years earlier in discussions during the time of the congregational evaluation. The pastor observed that "God's patience is a combination of compassion and urgency. God practices long periods of patience followed by an urgency [to act]. We need to implement this same kind of patience in the church."

The lay leadership and pastor of Weatherford Memorial Baptist Church graciously shared their recollections and insights with me, another example of the continuing legacy the members and leaders of this congregation gladly give so that others may benefit. The magnitude of their generosity is evident in these comments describing the closing service at Weatherford Memorial:

> During Weatherford's September 25, 2005, morning worship service Dr. Hurst presented the deed to the church property and buildings, valued at between $2 million and $2.25 million, to Dr. Lance Watson, senior pastor of the exploding St. Paul's church. It was not sold to St. Paul's. It was a gift from one Richmond Baptist Association church to a sister association church.[5]

THE CASE OF BAINBRIDGE STREET BAPTIST CHURCH

Bainbridge Street Baptist Church began as the Manchester Baptist Church, constituted on April 26, 1857, in what was then the town of Manchester in Chesterfield County on the south side of the James River adjacent to Richmond, Virginia.[6] William E. Hatcher served as the second pastor, from 1858–1867, and David B. Winfree as the fourth, from 1873–1879. These two men would become historic leaders in Virginia Baptist life. The members of Manchester faced the hardships of the Civil War and its aftermath. Blanche Syndor White wrote about "problems caused by poverty and the nervous exhaustion of a people who had fought a losing battle against superior forces, a people who at the close of four years of civil war had endured the bitterness of defeat, the humiliation of martial law, the drudgery of reconstruction."[7]

Yet the congregation survived and by 1880 voted to establish a mission and purchase property for a Baptist church in "Swansboro, a village just beyond the western limits of the city [of Manchester]."[8] Within a year, this mission church would become Clopton Street Baptist Church. With the organization of this second Baptist church in the Manchester-Swansboro area, Manchester Baptist Church chose to assume the name Bainbridge Street Baptist Church.[9]

Bainbridge Street continued to be an influential part of Baptist life in South Richmond. Over the years, as the population grew southward from Richmond, Bainbridge Street facilitated the establishment of new congregations including Stockton Street Baptist Church (1892), Oak Grove Baptist Church (1897), and Webber Memorial Baptist Church (1922). In 1907, members of Clopton Street Baptist Church, the first mission sponsored by Bainbridge Street, disagreed about relocating their church. This disagreement resulted in a group leaving to form Weatherford Memorial Baptist Church, the last congregation whose roots can be traced to Bainbridge Street Baptist Church.

In his introductory comments to *A Century of Service: A History of Bainbridge Street Baptist Church, 1857–1957*,

Dr. Russell T. Cherry Jr., pastor in 1957, made the following observation: "It is a poor sort of person who can take all the treasures of yesterday without feeling that he owes some obligation to the future. We, of course, feel a living bond, between us and the past, but, at the same time, we feel a sense of kinship with the long future."[10] The members of Bainbridge Street Baptist Church struggled to maintain their identity and role as a force for Baptist life in South Richmond for almost fifty more years. Ultimately, the congregation voted to sell the property and close the church in the fall of 2004.

I attempted to interview the pastor and key leaders of the congregation to learn about the process they followed in the closing months of the life of this once-dynamic church. Multiple calls to the former pastor were not returned; however, three influential former leaders of the congregation did agree to be interviewed. Each of these lay leaders had been a long-term member, one of whom was registered on the nursery roles as a child in 1932. Bainbridge Street was always his church home. All three served on the board of deacons during the last year of the church's existence.

I asked them to reflect on the moment when they realized that the church could not continue to exist. Each held a somewhat different view. The leader with the longest association with the church recalled that in the early to mid-1990s there had been discussion about closing the church. He was not in favor of the idea then and continued to remain resistant to any attempts to close the church even when the members finally voted to close Bainbridge Street in 2004.

He was keenly aware of the problems facing the congregation—the membership had continued to fall, expenses kept rising, and newer members were not able to support the budget. These financial issues were exacerbated by what he viewed as the excessively high cost of personnel. Salaries for the pastor, secretary, janitor, and organist had grown over the years to the point that a significant portion of the budget was dedicated to paying the staff.

A second lay leader became aware of the eventual need to close the church over time. He realized that the congregation was "staying open for themselves." In earlier years they had served the community with active food pantry and clothes closet ministries, but no longer. The church had even merged with Southampton Baptist Church for more than ten years, trying to be "one church in two locations." This relationship eventually dissolved when the two churches realized that they had never truly become one. This leader felt that the church's situation became a matter of good stewardship of their individual and collective resources. Their financial resources could be used better in healthy churches where not as much would be spent for maintenance and upkeep of an old facility.

The third lay leader never wanted to admit that the church would not survive and continued to hold out hope, in spite of the many challenges the congregation faced. When a designated gift was used to install an elevator, while routine maintenance work was neglected, he finally admitted to himself that the church was not going to make it. He, too, felt the church was spending too much money on personnel. Salaries and benefits amounted to more than 50 percent of the annual budget. New members did not contribute sufficient funds to help support the expensive personnel.

Early in 2004, the members of Bainbridge Street voted to sell the church property and close the church. All three of these key leaders served on the board of deacons that made this recommendation to the congregation. Each had expressed some ongoing reticence to close. When asked to tell what they did to make the process of closing the church move forward more smoothly, one explained that he did not do much during the last months. His wife was terminally ill, thus he devoted virtually all of his time to her care.

A second leader remembered encouraging the members to share their concerns with him openly. During the congregational meeting held to discuss closing the church, the members had considered options including relocating, joining with another congregation in a merger, and closing. Following this meeting, he had stayed to listen to members' questions and explore these options with them.

The third leader with whom I spoke had initially not been in favor of closing the church, but once the decision was made to sell the property, he was supportive. He tried to "open the eyes of other members and help them see what steps needed to be taken." The congregation's first choice had been to sell the property to another church in the hope that a vital ministry might once again take place in that location. Subsequently, he had assisted in acquiring an appraisal and selecting an agent to market the property.

Bainbridge Street did sell the property to another church and offered to hold the mortgage. A committee was established to oversee the receipt and distribution of these proceeds to designated recipients. When the original purchaser sold the property to another religious organization, the mortgage was paid in full. When all assets had been liquidated, well over $400,000 was available for distribution.

Each of these Bainbridge Street leaders believed that he had helped other members move ahead. They contributed to a relatively smooth transition by remaining open to questions and suggestions, by listening to members' concerns, and by following the instructions members had given concerning the disposition of the property. When asked what they would do differently, the interviewee who had never given up hope that the church would survive remained unswerving, insisting that he should have been more vocal in encouraging the church to remain open and delay closure longer. The other two leaders did not believe they should have done anything differently.

In response to my question seeking suggestions for other churches facing a similar situation, one leader felt that the letter sent by the board of deacons to members was a positive action other churches should consider. Another believed that contacting the local association for guidance was beneficial. The associational staff gave the leaders at Bainbridge Street suggestions and helped them see their situation more clearly.

With so many issues to address during the closing months of a church, the possibility that something might divert the attention of the members or leaders from the task is quite real. When asked if there were any such diversions with which Bainbridge Street had to contend, one leader believed that once the congregation made the decision, their attention remained focused.

Another highlighted what he perceived to be a significant issue during the last six months. The Wednesday night programs were directed at the younger people in the community, while no support or understanding was extended to the older members who were struggling with the issues of closing. All believed that helping members prepare for life after the church closes is essential. This might involve providing information about other churches where they might attend. The process of closing a congregation is more painful for some than others. Careful attention and appropriate support needs to be given to members who are having the greatest difficulty with the closure.

Each leader was asked if he could imagine a "perfect way" that a church might bring its ministry to an end. One of the leaders could envision another church that truly wanted to come in and "take over," assuming all responsibilities for the church, but allowing the present members to continue to worship there. In his view, this would mean that the members would not have to go through all the hurt.

One leader thought a process similar to what they had done could be used, with only slight improvement. Although Bainbridge Street held a special closing service, he believed that holding an appreciation event to celebrate the life of the church would have been valuable. This event could have included a catered meal, to relieve members of the responsibilities of food preparation, service, and cleanup. All members could have been encouraged to bring their scrapbooks, pictures, and memorabilia to share and reminisce with one another.

The remaining leader thought they had handled the closure well. The Bainbridge Street members wanted the property sold to another church so that it would continue to be used for ministry. This task had been accomplished in keeping with the members' wishes.

I asked each of these leaders if there was one thing that they would absolutely do again. Their responses were varied. One leader shared his concern for the inactive members the church had been unable to reach. He would have made an extra effort to contact them, even if it had required visiting them personally.

Another felt strongly that it was essential to provide financial support to the Virginia Baptist Historical Society following the sale of the church. The society was given the historical documents and materials recounting the history of Bainbridge Street. He believed this contribution would ensure that Bainbridge Street Baptist Church would not be forgotten.

The third leader emphasized the importance of establishing the fund for the distribution of the church's financial assets. Soon after the vote to close the church was taken, the congregation approved a plan for distributing the proceeds from the sale of the property and elected a committee to manage these funds. In addition to the Virginia Baptist Historical Society, the recipients included two International Mission Board missionaries, the Richmond Baptist Association, the Virginia Baptist Children's Home, and the Virginia Baptist Foundation.

I inquired whether there was anything that these leaders would absolutely not do again. One simply would not want to go through the process ever again. A second believed the closing event was a celebration, but he felt the church should not have spent the extra money to hold the event. The third leader would not have been so vocal after the decision was made to close. He had refused to "give it up," and felt he had always rubbed people the wrong way. He would not do that again. He admitted, "Once the decision is made, you need to let it go."

In reflecting on the importance of the time Bainbridge Street had taken to close, each leader held a different view. One leader felt, "Ten months to a year from the time it is voted on is plenty of time." He believed that it was a smooth process, noting that the closing need not occur on a particular date, such as an anniversary. "When you are finished with the process, go ahead and close." Another felt that Bainbridge Street had taken too much time. He believed that a couple of months would have been sufficient. The last

leader thought that such a process requires more than a
year. The church needed time to work through things, especially for the long-term members. "Be deliberate and don't
be too hasty," he advised. "Pray on things; prayer is very
important."

In the intervening years, the Bainbridge Street property
has continued in transition. The original purchaser intended
to open a Christian school on the property. Unforeseen
building issues prevented them from securing the necessary
authorization from the city. Eventually, the property was
sold to another church and is once again being used for worship and ministry.

THE CASE OF 23RD AND BROADWAY BAPTIST CHURCH

Deborah Carlton Loftis began her ministry at 23rd and
Broadway Baptist Church in Louisville, Kentucky, as the
minister of music in 1982. When she accepted the part-time
position, she did not think she was going to a dying congregation, but rather a church that was trying to redefine itself
in light of its changing context. By the end of her three years
at 23rd and Broadway, the church had disbanded as a congregation and sold their property to another congregation.
In the closing months of the life of 23rd and Broadway,
Dr. Loftis also served as the associate pastor. In these capaci-
ties, she journeyed with the congregation as they deliberated
and made decisions. When the church concluded its ministry, she was there to provide support and guidance for the
members.

Dr. Loftis shared with me that the church had begun in
the late nineteenth century in another location in the city.
When it moved to 23rd and Broadway, it changed its name
to reflect its location. Through the 1950s, it had been a

rather conservative, blue-collar congregation with a fairly large membership. In the 1960s, the church made the first of two significant commitments that would redefine and reshape its future. The residential community around the church experienced a transition as African Americans moved into the area. The congregation decided to embrace their new neighbors and welcomed all who wished to join in worship. One consequence of this decision was that the church became active in the civil rights movement in Louisville. Another was that many of the original members left the congregation. The 1970s saw a second controversial commitment when the church called a husband and wife to be co-pastors. Once again, a significant number of members left the church.

These two decisions reflected the congregation's willingness to take a position on what it meant for them to live out the gospel. They redefined who could be a member of their church and who could be a minister in their church. This represented a bold embodiment of the congregation's understanding of what they believed it meant to be the body of Christ.

Not long after Dr. Loftis assumed her position as minister of music, the church entered into a long-range visioning process with Dr. Robert Dale. Dr. Dale was, at that time, professor of Pastoral Leadership and Church Ministries at Southeastern Baptist Theological Seminary in Wake Forest, North Carolina. He had just completed his fourth book, *To Dream Again.*[11]

At the conclusion of this long-range planning process with Dr. Dale, the staff and members who were involved in "visioning" the future of their church came to the realization that their church "may need to die." This was a surprising outcome for almost everyone at 23rd and Broadway, according to Loftis. Like many dying congregations who engage in long-range planning, the members of 23rd and Broadway may have anticipated that the process would produce strategies that would reverse the church's decline.

Extensive conversations ensued. By the time the church met in business session, most of the people had come to believe that the best way for the church to live out the gospel was to let the church die. In their view, it was more important to preserve the gospel than it was to preserve the institution. A major portion of their resources was being expended just to keep the building from deteriorating further. To the members, doing the gospel meant more than devoting their financial resources to maintaining the building. Dr. Dale's leadership and the congregation's work during the visioning process were the catalysts that enabled the members and Dr. Loftis to see this choice more clearly. Everyone realized that it would be hard work, but the members agreed that they had done hard things before and they could do this. I could not help marveling at the depth of faith their decision demonstrated.

Dr. Loftis shared that some of the members wanted to start a new church in another location. Others no longer felt they had the energy or physical resources to start over in a new location. The interim pastor agreed to go with the members who wanted to start a new church. Dr. Loftis recalled making an intentional choice to remain with the members who did not want to start over. The members voted to sell the church to another congregation that needed a building so that a Christian ministry would continue in that location. Twenty-third and Broadway Baptist Church was disbanded, and members were given the freedom to transfer their membership to another congregation or join the new church. Funds were set aside and a committee formed to oversee the distribution of financial support for the new church start.

Those who chose to remain turned their attention to finding a congregation that needed a building and preparing for the transfer of the property. While they went through this process, they also devoted time to looking back. Dr. Loftis shared with me the many ways they provided for remembering and celebrating the history of the church. Each worship service included time for remembering people, events, and special occasions.

The members who remained behind began the huge process of cleaning and preparing the church for transfer to a new congregation. Those who were starting the new church were given the opportunity to select items they wanted to take for use in their new setting. All members were able to purchase items for a token amount to take home. Dr. Loftis described how, throughout this process, the members intentionally took time to remember these objects, their significance in the life of the congregation, and the persons for whom the items held special meaning.

During the final week, two services were held. Dr. Loftis described the first as a private, members-only service held in their small worship area on the last Wednesday night. The members gathered in a circle, and each was served Communion by the ministers. This was an emotional and meaningful service. The final worship service was held on Sunday. Between 300 and 400 people, including many former pastors, attended this celebration of the life of 23rd and Broadway Baptist Church.

Dr. Loftis believed her efforts helped the members of 23rd and Broadway who stayed until the church closed. She sensed that her choice to remain with them rather than to seek another position, or go with the new church start group, may have helped diminish the guilt felt by some who remained. The time she took to help the members intentionally remember and honor the past was meaningful for them. Dr. Loftis affirmed the members' desires to use their assets to continue ministry in some fashion. They accomplished this by establishing scholarships at a seminary and an African-American college, and by funding other ministry efforts. Listening and helping members deal with their memories and treating them gently helped them through those difficult days.

In reflecting on what she might have done differently, two particular issues surfaced. Dr. Loftis felt that being more intentional about maintaining contact with the disbursed members would have been ideal. Spending more time in self-care would also have been helpful. She believes that clergy who engage in such efforts could benefit from the help of a professional counselor.

I asked Dr. Loftis to mention things she thought other churches facing this situation ought to do. Her immediate response was "taking time to remember." This was an important and meaningful component of her efforts with the congregation.

A second suggestion was the use of an outside consultant as a congregational resource. Dr. Bill Leonard, then professor of Church History at Southern Baptist Theological Seminary in Louisville, Kentucky, had once served as their interim pastor. He spoke with the congregation, verifying that the members had done some things well. He reminded them that they had embraced a wider diversity in the congregation and opened their pulpit to women. His comments encouraged and affirmed their efforts over the years. Dr. Loftis recalls, "He helped them understand that 'failing' and 'dying' are not the same things; that sometimes when you succeed, it kills you."

When I asked Dr. Loftis what had helped her personally to move forward toward closure of the church, she remembered that it was a gradual process. Having come to the church only months before the visioning process started, she did not have the same emotional engagement as most of the members she served. She remembered that at the time it seemed to be the only decision to make, as expenses mounted and resources dwindled.

"Telling their stories," Dr. Loftis said, "helped them move on." She recalled how important it was to sit and let members deal with whatever they needed to process. Working at the church during that time "felt like serving a congregation where every single member had a terminal illness."

From Dr. Loftis's perspective, there is no one perfect way to conclude the ministry of a congregation. "Each congregation is unique. What would be perfect for one might not be perfect for another," she said. There are several key things she would look for in the process:

• Honoring the past.
• Providing each member a way into the future. She had encouraged each member to make a decision about what congregation he or she would join.
• Doing something constructive with the assets when the church can no longer use them.
• Providing pastoral care for members to let them know it is okay to be angry, to be hurt, and to be scared.

Dr. Loftis saw this process as similar to the way a family would deal with a terminal illness. I could certainly identify with that description of her experience. I felt I had been experiencing this same emotion with my own congregation, and they had not yet openly acknowledged the state of their congregational health.

Of all the activities that were part of the closing of 23rd and Broadway, there was one that Dr. Loftis would absolutely repeat. The Wednesday night members-only Communion service was, without question, a memorable event for the congregation and staff alike. When asked about what might have been done differently, she wished the new congregation could have received more freedom to use the funds set aside for them rather than dealing with a committee that exerted control over the distribution of those monies.

Eighteen months passed between the day the church voted to close and disband and the day the final service was held. Dr. Loftis believed they needed at least a year to handle the sale of the building, to dispose of the contents, and to grieve and celebrate. Eighteen months allowed time to be intentional, to plan, and to provide members with the care and attention they needed. "But there does come a time when you just have to let go," she explained.

THE CASE OF CALVARY BAPTIST CHURCH

Calvary Baptist Church had been a part of the historic Fan District of Richmond, Virginia, for many years before Dr. Elmer West came as their pastor. The church had been established in a working-class neighborhood. Steps led up from the street to the main floor and sanctuary. At the time of Calvary's construction, there was little need to provide parking for parishioners. Most walked from their homes to the church. In time, accessibility became an increasingly

more critical issue for the aging congregation. External circumstances were not kind to the church. The construction
of the Downtown Expressway split the neighborhood, isolat-
ing some in the community and displacing others.
Gradually, the area changed from a residential neighborhood
to an urban business environment.

In 1986 the church called on Dr. West to serve as their
pastor. He had served there as an interim pastor once before.
Dr. West told me that during his previous tenure, he had
estimated the average age of the congregation at eighty-two.
When he received this call, he presented the church with a
proposal. He would come as their pastor, committing to a
three-year contract, if the congregation would agree to
merge with another church or disband at the end of the
three-year period. Dr. West knew the church's context, their
history, and their membership. Not all pastors are fortunate
enough to have the kind of prior knowledge and experience
that Dr. West brought to this situation. The members and
leaders of Calvary knew Dr. West as well. The congregation
accepted his proposal, and they enjoyed three satisfying years
working together.

Dr. West shared with me that he allowed about eighteen
months to pass before he began conversations with the key
leadership, insisting that they needed to work toward merger
or closure. The church formed a Future Planning
Committee and began a dialogue with what was then Park
View Baptist Church, located on Patterson Avenue in
Richmond. The pastor and leadership of Park View were
open to the concept of merger, and serious discussion
ensued. The merger went smoothly and concluded with the
two congregations becoming what is now Patterson Avenue
Baptist Church. The Calvary Baptist Church property was
sold to developers and eventually converted into business

space. The pastor of Park View Baptist Church continued to serve as pastor of the newly created Patterson Avenue Baptist Church for two years after the merger.

Dr. West told me that several key factors made the process flow smoothly. The first was the selection of the Future Planning Committee. A second critical element was the support provided by one of the most influential and respected members of the congregation. This individual, along with Dr. West and the deacons, selected the six members of the Future Planning Committee. With this committee in place and committed to the task, Dr. West turned his attention to two other prominent members of the congregation whom he thought might be opposed to a merger. In private meetings with these individuals, Dr. West learned that one was in favor of the merger and had been working behind the scenes to ensure financial resources would be available to support the expanded ministry of the soon-to-be-created congregation. The second person remained resistant to the idea until the church officially voted to merge, at which point all reluctance ceased. Dr. West's actions confirmed what I suspected—that engaging in dialogue with the influential and respected members early in the process was critical to success. (See the "Leadership Assessment" tool in the appendix. This may be helpful in specifically identifying the influential and respected members in your own congregation.)

Dr. West shared how he never missed an opportunity to talk about the merger during sermons and on other occasions in the life of the congregation. He summed up his view of the process with this keen observation: "It was the right time and the right place and the right people." All of these factors contributed to the successful transition from two congregations into one new entity. I wondered if there had been any resistance to the merger from the membership of Park View. Dr. West knew of none. He felt this may have been due, in part, to the thoughtful planning of that key financial figure at Calvary who had set aside a significant amount of Calvary's resources to help ease any burden the new members would place on Park View's budget.

When I asked Dr. West whether he would do things differently if he had to do it over again, he thought that he and the church would handle things the same way they had back then. Again, he attributed the smooth transition to "the right time, the right place, and the right people." Without the support and leadership of key people within the congregation, things would probably not have gone as well.

Although he was too modest to state the obvious, the role Dr. West played could not have been more crucial to the process either. The contractual agreement between Dr. West and the congregation was an important first step. In his view, this is an approach churches facing a similar situation should consider. Dr. West confessed that he had witnessed the alternative—churches entering into codependency relationships with pastors. "When a church is struggling to remain viable, often they cannot attract the youngest and brightest pastors." Instead, churches often select older pastors seeking to serve out their ministry years and retire. This contributes to a relationship where risk and challenge are uncomfortable and threatening. Maintaining the status quo becomes the objective. By reaching an agreement at the beginning of the relationship with the pastor, churches can avoid this problem.

I was curious about whether anything had diverted the members' attention from the task of concluding their ministry during those last months. Dr. West believed that the intentional approach he took with Calvary may have helped them avoid situations that could have diverted them from the ultimate achievement of the merger with the Park View congregation. The last three years were times of good music and good preaching, even though there were few outside guests or special activities. Dr. West recalled that he preached on missions and focused on opportunities to support and encourage foreign mission endeavors.

Confirming what I had heard from others, Dr. West could not imagine any single, perfect way to end a church's ministry. Each situation would be different, with different personalities and issues. In his view, perhaps the most important component of the process for other churches facing closure would be to have the support and involvement of influential and respected congregational leaders. Although these people may hold important offices or have key roles in the church, this may not be the case at all. They may simply be the people to whom others look for counsel and advice. You know those people in your church. They are the individuals to whom everyone turns during controversial votes in business meetings. How those individuals vote often determines the success or failure of the question.

The process of merger took three years for Calvary Baptist Church. This timeframe was intentional and predetermined. Dr. West believed that three years was the right amount of time for Calvary, but he hastened to add that "each church is unique."

SUMMARY

During all the interviews I conducted, I was universally impressed by everyone's openness to tell their stories and share their experiences. Both laity and clergy readily confided their reflections on what may have been a difficult and painful time. They participated with nothing more than a

desire to share so that other churches might somehow benefit from their experiences. They hoped that by sharing their
experiences, they might help other churches enter into a
similar process better informed about some of the issues they
would encounter.

Each of the congregational situations exhibited unique
characteristics. There were also common features that had a
positive influence on the congregations as they concluded
their active ministries. These factors included
- an accurate assessment of the congregation's vitality;
- the support and involvement of congregational leaders;
- pastoral leadership;
- a process for remembering and honoring the past;
- the provision of sufficient time and opportunities for
  members to engage in the process; and
- attention to and provision for life after closure.

As I look at this list of factors, I cannot help reflecting on
my own parishioners and how much I was reminded of
them in the conversations I had with the leaders of these
closed congregations. They all loved their churches. They all
longed for that lost time when their congregation was vital,
growing, and thriving. The difference seemed to lie in the
inability of Southampton leaders to "look down." Or, in
looking down, they were unable to focus on the reality.
There is a need for these common features to be present
within a congregation that is facing the end. In the final
chapter, I will share more about these and other elements
discovered during my interviews with those who have been
through the process.

Questions to Consider

1. Are leaders open to exploring the question of the church's viability? Are the members open? The ministerial staff? On a scale of 1 to 5, with 1 being completely closed to discussion and 5 being completely open, how would you rank each group?

2. What can you do to encourage more openness and dialogue about the church's viability?

3. What can your congregation learn from the case of Weatherford Memorial? From Bainbridge Street? From 23rd and Broadway? From Calvary?

Notes

1. Alice Mann, *Can Our Church Live?: Redeveloping Congregations in Decline* (Bethesda MD: The Alban Institute, 1999) 8.

2. Beth Ann Gaede, *Ending with Hope: A Resource for Closing Congregations* (Bethesda MD: The Alban Institute, 2002) vi–vii.

3. Nancy R. Elliott and Alberta L. Lindsey, *A Living Legacy: The Church Which Gave Itself Away* (Richmond, 2007) 16.

4. Ibid., 43.

5. Ibid., 77.

6. Blanche Syndor White, *A Century of Service: A History of Bainbridge Street Baptist Church, 1857–1957* (Richmond: Whittet and Shepperson, 1956) 26.

7. Ibid., 50.

8. Ibid., 69.

9. Ibid., 70.

10. Ibid., 7–8.

11. Robert D. Dale, *To Dream Again* (Nashville: Broadman Press, 1981).

## Chapter 4

SHARED WISDOM FOR THE PATH AHEAD

In the eight months I spent collecting information and interviewing the people who had been involved in closing four churches, another 1,600 churches might well have closed in America.[1] I began this endeavor with lots of questions. I was convinced that congregational leaders who had participated in the closure of a church had acquired knowledge that could be helpful. You probably have some of the same questions I had back then.

- What combinations of care and nurture work best in a dying congregation?
- What forms of worship and preaching work well?
- What education and self-study programs assist the members of dying churches to come to terms with their situation and then move forward while appropriately honoring their past?
- Is it possible that, in dying, churches might find ways to live on after the closing?
- What courses of action should be avoided if at all possible?

I did not find specific answers to all of these questions, but I did discover useful information. Perhaps the most heartening discovery was that I was not alone in my struggle to understand and communicate with others about the phenomenon I have come to know as the "dying congregation." Not surprisingly, I discovered that new life can come out of death.

Dying congregations necessitate a different kind of nurture and care than congregations in the *Adulthood* stage of congregational development (see Figure 1). The pastor of Weatherford Memorial came to understand this with the help of a seminary professor. What was true for Weatherford Memorial was also true, in varying ways, for each of the other congregations I had researched. Every dying congregation will require a unique combination of nurture, encouragement, challenge, and comfort. The pastor and key leaders are critical in discerning and implementing appropriate ministries for each distinct congregation.

Preaching and worship can provide congregations with opportunities to grow in their understanding of the nature of the church universal and their local church's role and responsibility as part of the larger community of faith. Through his sermons, the pastor of Calvary Baptist Church informed and challenged the members to focus on their future, not as that distinct congregation, but as participants in the broader church family. Sermons encouraged their support for foreign missions and their commitment to the upcoming merger with Park View Baptist.

At 23rd and Broadway Baptist Church, the pastor and leaders provided worship experiences that allowed their members to affirm the church's past and reflect on its future. Pastors of dying congregations can use their sermons to challenge and stretch as well as comfort and console. What works best will be unique for each congregation.

Twenty-third and Broadway and Weatherford Memorial both undertook a somewhat formal process of self-examination. Bainbridge Street and Calvary churches each engaged in their own approaches to self-discovery. In every situation, the process was instrumental in helping the congregation discern their present situation and chart a course for their future. Whether instituted by laity, by pastoral leadership, or at the recommendation and leadership of an outside consultant, programs of self-examination and discovery can contribute positively to the ability of the congregation to move forward. Meaningful self-study will allow churches to look at their historical record, highlight highs and lows, recall past successes, and honestly reflect on their present circumstances.

In one way or another, every one of the churches I researched gave itself away. Each of these congregations undertook deliberate acts of sacrifice, some more reticently than others, but deliberate nonetheless. Bainbridge Street distributed assets of more than $400,000 to mission and ministry causes. Calvary and 23rd and Broadway endowed multiple ministries and invested significantly in new church entities. Weatherford Memorial confirmed that it is entirely possible for churches to give themselves away unselfishly. By their actions, each of these congregations has witnessed the multiplication of their gifts in significant and measurable ways.

The experiences these pastors and leaders shared confirmed one of my early suspicions. These people possessed valuable knowledge that can inform the efforts of members, leaders, and pastors in dying congregations everywhere as they seek to understand and fulfill their roles.

LESSONS FOR LEADERS

I realized more clearly than ever the enormous capacity leaders have to influence the course of events in the lives of their churches. From recognizing that the church is in crisis, to choosing the course of action the church will follow, to concluding the church's ministry, leaders can facilitate or thwart the efforts of everyone within the faith community. This was clearly evident in the work of the leaders of Bainbridge Street and Weatherford Memorial who contributed immeasurably toward the final transition of their respective church properties to new ministry endeavors.

Lesson #1: Realize your influence on members' perception of the church. Not only can leaders influence the perception members have of the health and viability of the church, but they can often significantly shape those perceptions. During the last study team meeting at Southampton, when one respected leader declared, "I'm not ready to give up," the attitude of the group began to shift. From that point on, the conversation changed from a review of options, given the limited resources of the congregation, to seeking outside help to address the church's thirty-year decline.

In light of the realities shared by the outside consultant at Weatherford Memorial, one couple was determined to help the church return to its original vision—to be "a lighthouse to South Richmond." They continually encouraged the members to "keep the main thing the main thing," becoming that lighthouse again. When the opportunity with the St. Paul's congregation arose, it became clear that their vision could be realized. The vision became a reality when members, supported and encouraged by this couple and others, approved the proposal.

The board of deacons of Bainbridge Street, more than any other constituency within that church community, moved that congregation toward the faithful conclusion of their ministry. When one leader determined that "staying open for ourselves" was poor stewardship of their resources, his voice was heard clearly by those who had long valued his counsel.

Even a church's decision to participate in a self-study or congregational evaluation process, such as those undertaken by Weatherford Memorial and 23rd and Broadway, may depend on whether there is leadership support. Perhaps truer than at any other time in their lives, when congregations face uncertain futures, their leaders wield significant influence that should be exercised with great care. This influence can come through direct conversation and participation in the processes undertaken by the church. It can also come just as forcefully through the absence of leaders at key meetings and activities. Withholding support and involvement is often as effective as direct resistance.

Lesson #2: Give members a forum to discuss their concerns. Leaders who are willing to listen to members' concerns can smooth the process of closing a church, as the leaders so graciously did at Bainbridge Street. Members frequently need to share anger, pain, frustration, and anxiety about what lies ahead. By listening to members, making themselves available to discuss options, and sharing their honest assessments, these leaders allowed members to realize gradually the reality of their congregational situation.

It is important to offer a variety of settings in which members can talk and share. Some members may prefer to meet privately in their homes with leaders. Others may want to gather in small groups, either in the church or in members' homes. Having larger meetings where a wider audience can exchange information and discuss their feelings may appeal to others. The key is for leadership to be flexible and creative in the ways they address members' needs for discussion and dialogue.

Lesson #3: Offer members options for the future. Many members will look to or seek leaders to help them sort through the issues surrounding closure. Leaders can mend fences or build walls as they interact with members who look to them for guidance and counsel. In most cases, there are a variety of options available for consideration. Even if leaders have reached consensus on the desired course of action, openly discussing other options, and permitting time for members to consider personally and process these possibilities may lead to a much smoother transition.

This can be seen in the different but productive approaches taken by 23rd and Broadway compared to Weatherford Memorial. In these churches, the leadership helped members consider options and make choices that best met their individual and corporate needs.

LESSONS FOR MEMBERS

I realized too that not all members of dying congregations are old. There is a difference, however, between being "old" and "aging." Many dying congregations can accurately be described as "aging." The members may not be old, but they can display an "aging" mindset. I found Martin Saarinen's description of a congregation in the *Aging* stage of the life cycle helpful.

> The congregation that had been energized in its search of the "holy grail"—however that may have been perceived

in the corporate vision or sense of mission—has lost its
ability to become energized by new opportunities. It has
lost the romance of being on the way, on the move,
pioneering; instead, the need for something sure and certain generates a kind of canonical mentality in which the
pursuit of what should be displaces the pursuit of what
could be.[2]

How often had I heard the phrase "we should be . . ." in
my congregation? Those who voice this view are often lifelong members who are dedicated and faithful folks. Having
watched changes taking place in the broader community
and within their beloved church home, they have come to
value the "sure and certain." They have worshiped, worked,
and worried as they have witnessed the decline in the vitality
of their church. Some members who are, in fact, older have
become increasingly less able to contribute, both physically
and financially. Regardless of their age, these lifelong members frequently wield tremendous power within the church
and loathe relinquishing or sharing it, especially with those
new to the congregation.

Lesson #1: Denial cannot bring renewal. My experience
at Southampton Baptist Church attested to these "aging"
characteristics. Although "worn out from years of serving
the church," Southampton's leaders continued to resist
the assessment that the church was dying. They chose to dis-
continue dialogue with their outside consultant rather than
consider alternatives that might lead to merger or dissolution.

Members of a dying congregation have responsibilities
that are crucial for the church's future. One of their foremost
challenges can be their ability to cultivate a spirit of honesty

with one another and with their lay and pastoral leadership. Denial of the realities facing them will likely have negative consequences. One of the leaders of Bainbridge Street recalled, with regret, his steadfast resistance to closing the church. Precious time, energy, and money may have been spent prolonging decisions. Only after the members of Weatherford Memorial came to a clear understanding of their situation were they able to chart their final course of action. That course conserved their remaining assets and permitted the maximization of their resources. The consequences of denial for any dying congregation may include the needless loss of financial and human capital.

Lesson #2: Listen to and talk with leaders and staff within the church. In the absence of a culture of openness within a dying congregation, pastoral and lay leadership may attempt to create one. The degree to which members embrace or reject this spirit will have a direct impact on their future. A willingness to participate in church-wide assessment and evaluation activities can enhance the possibilities for developing a healthier climate. These activities can contribute to the congregation's understanding of past events and current issues. This was certainly the case at Weatherford Memorial where members became better equipped to make honest assessments and realistic choices. Perhaps there is no clearer demonstration of the potential benefit of this dialogue than the legacy of Weatherford Memorial Baptist Church, who gave their property, valued at more than $2 million, to St. Paul's Baptist Church.

Lesson #3: Give yourself permission to grieve. Losing something you love is a painful. This is as true of the loss of an institution, a church, as it is of the loss of a personal relationship. Finding healthy ways to express our sadness and hurt is critical for our well-being. What I learned was that wrestling with these issues as a congregation was a grief process. Recognizing this process and giving support and encouragement to one another can contribute to a more positive outcome for all. In the midst of this, members must find ways of remembering and honoring the past, as the leadership and members of 23rd and Broadway did. As the members cleaned and readied the property for transfer, they took time to reflect on meaningful objects, significant times, and the people who had contributed to their life together. Their efforts allowed them to remain focused on the difficult work of concluding the ministry of the church, all the while honoring and celebrating their past life together.

LESSONS FOR PASTORS

Decisive pastoral leadership is essential. The leaders of both Bainbridge Street and Weatherford Memorial did not hesitate to share their views on the roles their pastors had played as the churches concluded their ministries. When pastoral leadership is absent, members and leaders notice the absence. When pastoral leadership is present, it is affirmed and appreciated. I have come to understand more clearly than ever the vital role of the pastor in dying congregations.

Lesson #1: Foster a spirit of healthy self-discovery. Creating an atmosphere in which members are willing to engage in a process of self-study and discernment is important at every stage in the life of a congregation. However, self-awareness for the dying congregation is of utmost importance. No one is more critical to this process than the pastor. The pastor of Weatherford Memorial saw the necessity of self-discovery for his congregation. He came to understand his encouragement of this process as part of his pastoral role. The likelihood of a congregation choosing to initiate such an undertaking without the support and encouragement of the pastor is remote.

The pastor at Calvary Baptist Church made it clear to that congregation that he would only accept the call as their pastor if they agreed to his proposal either to merge with another congregation or to disband after three years. Such an undertaking without the agreement of the leadership of the congregation is equally unlikely.

Pastoral leadership is critical in accomplishing this basic step of self-assessment. The pastor's role in interpreting the information gained from these efforts cannot be overstated. As unpleasant and challenging as this task may be for the pastor, congregations desperately need the support, encouragement, guidance, and interpretive skills of their pastors as they work through this process.

Lesson #2: Do not attempt to go it alone. Pastors are wise to seek and engage the support of congregational leaders in this process. The pastor of Calvary embodied this role well. Equipping and encouraging leaders in the nurture and care of the members during the process of closure is equally crucial. The pastor must cast a vision of the future for leaders and members alike. Having a small group of core leaders with whom to dialogue, share, and plan will spread the load of congregational leadership. This can free the pastor to concentrate on casting the vision through sermons, small group meetings, Bible study lessons, and committee meetings. The pastor more than anyone else can continually focus the congregation on the task ahead.

Beyond their congregation, pastors can benefit from meeting with colleagues, individually or in small groups, with denominational leaders, or with outside consultants.

My personal experience in meeting with denominational and associational leaders, and with colleagues, helped provide invaluable insight in my efforts with my congregation.

Lesson #3: Plan for the future. An essential part of the pastoral care of the congregation is preparation for life after the church has closed, merged with another congregation, or relocated. The work of the associate pastor of 23rd and Broadway in this regard is noteworthy. She sought to provide each member with a way into the future by encouraging everyone to make a decision about what congregation he or she would join. This task is particularly important when a congregation is closing and disbanding, as opposed to merging. By providing contact information, arranging presentations, and encouraging visits to other churches, the pastor can facilitate the transition of members from one congregation to another.

Some members will have clear ideas about the church they would like to attend, while others may be at a complete loss. Members may need to have permission to visit and try out other churches before their own church officially closes. This process can be informal or highly structured. Congregational leaders can be of assistance in organizing a variety of opportunities for members to plan for their future church participation.

LESSONS FOR EVERYONE

I have found that one of the best ways for me to learn is by repetition. In the course of my conversations with congregational leaders and clergy alike, I began to hear some things over and over again.

Lesson #1: Seek the counsel of knowledgeable, outside consultants. Foremost in the minds of many of those who shared their stories was the conviction that the counsel of outside consultants was invaluable. The leaders of Weatherford Memorial mentioned this frequently. Consultants can offer their observations candidly, without a personal agenda or any selfish motivation. They can speak prophetically, often in ways that congregational members are not able to speak. Furthermore, they can bring new ideas and opportunities to the congregation.

Members, leaders, and pastors who seek and welcome the assistance of consultants, as Weatherford and 23rd and Broadway did, will likely find their efforts rewarded. The connection between Weatherford Memorial and St. Paul's Baptist Church happened because the consultant knew of the needs of both congregations and was able to bring the two together. In an atmosphere of mutual respect, patience, and prayer, issues can often be identified, discussed, and resolved more readily.

Lesson #2: Timing is critical. Timing is a key element. During a church's final days, everyone seems to have a unique sense of the passage of time. The challenge is to ensure that sufficient time is taken so that all can work through the process without feeling forced or hurried. When this is achieved, it will ultimately promote a smoother transition toward closure. Weatherford Memorial and Bainbridge Street took the time necessary to their unique situations before holding their final services. Each congregation must wrestle with this issue and determine what works for them. Congregational leaders, members, and staff must engage in the conversation, recognizing that compromise is necessary.

Remembering and honoring the past, as represented by the artifacts and amenities of the church, affords everyone the best opportunity to participate in the process positively. Twenty-third and Broadway accomplished this well by the variety of opportunities given their members, including setting aside time during regularly scheduled worship services, holding special services, and providing time during smaller group gatherings. What worked well for them may not work well for another congregation. Be open, creative, and sensitive to the needs of your unique congregational situation.

Lesson #3: End well. I discovered considerable variation among the churches with respect to their closing services. A formal, public service of closure, marking the end of the active ministry of the church, can help the members acknowledge and honor their service to one another and to the broader community. The final worship of Weatherford Memorial models one such formal service. Weatherford's decision to create a legacy by giving themselves away to St. Paul's Baptist Church set the tone for a celebratory service that honored the past and looked forward to the future of the new congregation.

A congregation may want to have a more exclusive, private service just for current members as was done by 23rd and Broadway. This can be a meaningful and significant event for the members of a congregation who have labored through the difficult process. Emotions and feelings that a larger gathering might inhibit can be shared in a private setting.

Each congregation that shared experiences with me ultimately left a legacy upon the conclusion of their ministries. Some gave financially to empower ongoing ministries. Others invested in the birth and life of a new congregation

formed by the merger of two congregations, by transplanting a core group that blossomed into a new congregation, or
by a complete transformation and rebirth. Each closing congregation experienced the pangs of loss, and each felt a small
measure of the joy of giving birth to something new.
Whatever the future holds for a congregation, do not neglect
the importance of ending well.

EPILOGUE

The church universal, as the body of Christ, is a living and
holy organism and an organizational entity. So, too, is the
local congregation. The local congregation comes into being
by God's power and grace. Yet most church members give
little thought to the congregation as an organization with a
life span. This needs to change.

The task of transforming congregations belongs to all—
pastors, denominational leaders, organizational scholars,
lay leaders, and individual members. The majority of
churchgoers in North America are aware of the plight of
congregations today: many virtually empty churches, dwindling budgets, shrinking ministries, and a growing sense of
disillusionment.

Congregations deserve to hear the truth. The death of a
congregation is not the same thing as failure. Out of death
can come new life and new ministries. This is evident in the
experiences of the churches I have described to you.

• The members of 23rd and Broadway Baptist Church
who moved on to form a new congregation were supported
financially by the resources set aside for their use. A new
church came into being in their former building, offering a
unique ministry to a changed and changing community.

• Weatherford Memorial's dream of being a lighthouse in their community is alive and flourishing in the thriving ministry of St. Paul's Baptist Church South. Coupled with this growing ministry, the former members who have dispersed to congregations throughout metropolitan Richmond, Virginia, are contributing their gifts, talents, and resources to the vital ministries of their new church homes.

• Calvary Baptist Church gifted the Baptist Theological Seminary at Richmond with financial resources in its formative years. Calvary's members who merged into the newly created Patterson Avenue Baptist Church became charter members of a new body of believers. The financial resources provided to this new church by Calvary undergirded their early years and eased the transition for everyone involved. On October 4, 2009, Patterson Avenue Baptist Church celebrated the twentieth anniversary of its founding.

• Bainbridge Street Baptist Church continues to support a variety of ministries and agencies, both in Richmond, Virginia, and throughout the world. As their members wished, their former property continues to be the source of vital ministry in that community. Some of their members disbursed to churches in the greater Richmond area. Others relocated to areas elsewhere in the state, further disbursing their gifts and resources while continuing to demonstrate their commitment to stewardship.

• In July 2007, I accepted a call to serve on the staff of Baptist Theological Seminary at Richmond. Southampton Baptist Church has continued under the leadership of a bivocational pastor. In June 2009, the congregation voted to share their facilities with an emerging congregation, beginning a new chapter in their ongoing life.

God calls the church to faithfulness, not to some form of humanly defined success. Difficult and painful as the task may have been, each of the congregations that concluded their ministries released God's transformative power afresh in our world. Craig Van Gelder observes, "The church is a people shaped by the redemptive reign of God. The church is not an end in itself. It has a distinct calling—to demonstrate the reality of God's redemptive power in the world."[3]

These congregations remind me that God calls the church into being and into the partnership work of redemption. These congregations bear witness to the transformative power of God to bring new and vibrant life where there was once death. The stories of these congregations continue to offer hope and encouragement to churches everywhere that seek to live out their call as a people who are being shaped and transformed by the One who declared, "I am the resurrection and the life. Those who believe in me, even though they die, will live, and everyone who lives and believes in me will never die" (John 11:25-26).

Questions to Consider

1. List the leaders in your congregation. Are their positions on congregational viability known to the staff, other leaders, and the membership? Use the "Leadership Assessment" tool in the appendix to record this information.
2. On a scale of 1 to 5 (1 being in total denial and 5 being ready to move forward), assess the members' readiness to discuss the viability and future of the church.
3. On a scale of 1 to 5, how decisive is the pastoral leadership of your congregation?
4. What action(s) might it be time for your church to take?

Notes

1. Gilson A. C. Waldkoenig, "Closing Churches in the Light of American Religious History," in *Ending with Hope: A Resource for Closing Congregations*, ed. Beth Ann Gaede (Bethesda MD: The Alban Institute, 2002) 39–40.

2. Martin F. Saarinen, *The Life Cycle of a Congregation*, An Alban Institute Publication (Washington DC: The Alban Institute, 1990) 15.

3. Craig Van Gelder, *The Essence of the Church: A Community Created by the Spirit* (Grand Rapids: Baker Books, 2000) 51.

BIBLIOGRAPHY

Allen, Ronald J. *Patterns of Preaching: A Sermon Sampler.* St. Louis: Chalice Press, 1998.

Ammerman, Nancy Tatom. *Studying Congregations: A New Handbook.* Nashville: Abingdon Press, 1998.

Bandy, Thomas G. *Coaching Change: Breaking Down Resistance, Building up Hope.* Nashville: Abingdon Press, 2000.

Barna, George. *Turn around Churches: How to Overcome Barriers to Growth and Bring New Life to an Established Church.* Ventura: Regal Books, 1993.

Barnes, Rebecca, and Lindy Lowry. "Special Report: The American Church in Crisis." *Outreach*, May/June 2006.

Barrett, Lois, Inagrace T. Dietterich, Darrell L. Guder, George R. Hunsberger, Alan J. Roxburgh, and Craig Van Gelder. *Missional Church: A Vision for the Sending of the Church in North America*, ed. Darrell L. Guder. Grand Rapids: W. B. Eerdmans Publishing Company, 1998.

Branson, Mark Lau. *Memories, Hopes, and Conversations: Appreciative Inquiry and Congregational Change.* Herndon: Alban Institute, 2004.

Bugg, Charles B. *Preaching and Intimacy: Preparing the Message and the Messenger.* Macon GA: Smyth & Helwys, 1999.

Bullard, George W., Jr. *Pursuing the Full Kingdom Potential of Your Congregation.* St. Louis: Lake Hickory Resources, 2005.

Crandall, Ronald K., and Herb Miller. *Turnaround Strategies for the Small Church*. Effective Church Series. Nashville: Abingdon Press, 1995.

Dale, Robert D. *To Dream Again*. Nashville: Broadman Press, 1981.

―――. *Pastoral Leadership: A Handbook of Resources for Effective Congregational Leadership*. Nashville: Abingdon Press, 1986.

―――. *Leadership for a Changing Church: Charting the Shape of the River*. Nashville: Abingdon Press, 1999.

Elliott, Nancy R., and Alberta L. Lindsey. *A Living Legacy: The Church Which Gave Itself Away*. Richmond, 2007.

Gaede, Beth Ann. *Ending with Hope: A Resource for Closing Congregations*. Bethesda MD: The Alban Institute, 2002.

Galindo, Israel. *The Hidden Lives of Congregations: Understanding Congregational Dynamics*. Herndon: Alban Institute, 2004.

Gopin, Marc. *Healing the Heart of Conflict: 8 Crucial Steps to Making Peace with Yourself and Others*. Rodale, 2004.

Graham, Billy. *The Pastor's Guide to Effective Preaching*. Kansas City: Beacon Hill Press of Kansas City, 2003.

Grenz, Stanley J. *Theology for the Community of God*. Grand Rapids: W. B. Eerdmans Publishing Company, 2000.

Hammond, Sue Annis. *The Thin Book of Appreciative Inquiry*. 2nd edition. Bend OR: Thin Book Publishing Co., 1998.

Hunter, George G., III. *How to Reach Secular People*. Nashville: Abingdon Press, 1992.

―――. *Church for the Unchurched*. Nashville: Abingdon Press, 1996.

Lamey, Paul. "Length of Tenure." 20 February 2006. http://expositorythoughts.wordpress.com/2006/02/20/l ength-of-tenure/ (accessed 13 February 2008).

Long, Thomas G. *Beyond the Worship Wars: Building Vital and Faithful Worship.* An Alban Institute Publication. Bethesda MD: The Alban Institute, 2001.

Lott, David B. *Conflict Management in Congregations.* Bethesda MD: Alban Institute, 2001.

Mann, Alice. *Can Our Church Live?: Redeveloping Congregations in Decline.* Bethesda MD: Alban Institute, 1999.

McLaren, Brian D. *The Church on the Other Side: Doing Ministry in the Postmodern Matrix.* Grand Rapids: Zondervan Publishing House, 2000.

Merriam, Sharan B. *Qualitative Research and Case Study Applications in Education.* San Francisco: Jossey-Bass Publishers, 1998.

Myers, William R. *Research in Ministry: A Primer for the Doctor of Ministry Program.* Third edition. Chicago: Exploration Press, 2002.

Nelson, Alan E. *Creating Messages That Connect: 10 Secrets of Effective Communicators.* Loveland CO: Group Publishing, Inc., 2004.

Richardson, Ronald W. *Creating a Healthier Church: Family Systems Theory, Leadership, and Congregational Life.* Creative Pastoral Care and Counseling Series. Minneapolis: Fortress Press, 1996.

Robinson, Anthony B., and Robert W. Wall. *Called to Be Church: The Book of Acts for a New Day.* Grand Rapids: W. B. Eerdmans Publishing Company, 2006.

Saarinen, Martin F. *The Life Cycle of a Congregation.* An Alban Institute Publication. Washington DC: The Alban Institute, 1990.

Steinke, Peter L. *Healthy Congregations: A Systems Approach.* Bethesda MD: Alban Institute, 1996.

Stevens, R. Paul, and Phil Collins. *The Equipping Pastor: A Systems Approach to Congregational Leadership.* Washington DC: Alban Institute, 1993.

Van Gelder, Craig. *The Essence of the Church: A Community Created by the Spirit.* Grand Rapids: Baker Books, 2000.

Watkins, Jane Magruder, and Bernard J. Mohr. *Appreciative Inquiry: Change at the Speed of Imagination.* San Francisco: Jossey-Bass/Pfeiffer, 2001.

White, Blanche Sydnor. *A Century of Service: A History of Bainbridge Street Baptist Church, 1857–1957.* Richmond: Whittet and Shepperson, 1956.

Willimon, William H. *The Last Word: Insights About the Church and Ministry.* Nashville: Abingdon Press, 2000.

Wilson, Charles Reagan, and Mark Silk. *Religion and Public Life in the South: In the Evangelical Mode.* Religion by Region. Walnut Creek CA: AltaMira Press, 2005.

APPENDIX

Each of the charts below is available as a downloadable PDF at
www.helwys.com/books/jenkins.html

Congregational Assessment

Church

Church Name	
Address	
City, State ZIP	
Denomination	
Affiliations/Associations	
Date Formed/Founded	
Original Location (if different from present)	
Current Pastor	
Date Started	
Total # of Pastorates	
Average tenure	

Membership

Membership on the church role											
Active membership											
Age range of active members											
# New members each year for last 10 years											
# Members lost each year for last 10 years											

Congregatinal Assessment (continued)

Worship and Sunday School/Bible Study

	Sun.	Mon.	Tues.	Wed.	Thur.	Fri.	Sat.
# Worship Services each week							
Scheduled Time							
Average attendance							
# Visitors							
# Bible studies (incl. Sunday School)							
Time							
Average attendance							
# Visitors							

Leadership

# Ministerial staff - full-time/part-time			
# Deacons/Elders/Lay ministers/Others			
# Team/Committee leaders			
# Teachers			

Leadership Assessment

Deacons/Elders

Name	Position	Elected or Appointed?	Degree of Influence with Members		
			Strong	Moderate	Slight

Teachers

Name	Position	Elected or Appointed?	Degree of Influence with Members		
			Strong	Moderate	Slight

Leadership Assessment (continued)

Lay Ministers/Leaders

Name	Position	Elected or Appointed?	Degree of Influence with Members		
			Strong	Moderate	Slight

Ministries Assessment

Current Ministries	How many involved (serving)?	# involved as % of total in category	Number served (recipients)	Cost as % of budget or income
Staff to members				
Members to members				
Members to local community				
Members to international/ overseas community				
Ministries 5 Years Ago				
Staff to members				
Members to members				
Members to local community				
Members to international/ overseas community				
Ministries 10 Years Ago				
Staff to members				
Members to members				
Members to local community				
Members to international/ overseas community				

Physical Plant Assessment

Area/Space	Condition/Appearance			Utilization		
	Good	Fair	Poor	Often	Occasional	Seldom
Sanctuary						
Classrooms						
Fellowship space						
Offices						
Storage						
Equipment						
Office						
Building & Grounds						

Physical Plant Assessment (continued)

Vehicles						
Mechanical systems						
HVAC						
Plumbing						
Electrical						
Exterior						
Building						
Playground						
Parking areas						
Other						